THE BOOK OF

JAPANESE
COOKING

THE BOOK OF

JAPANESE
COOKING

EMI KAZUKO

Photographed by
SIMON BUTCHER

HPBooks

ANOTHER BEST SELLING VOLUME FROM HP BOOKS

HPBooks
Published by The Berkley Publishing Group
200 Madison Avenue
New York, NY 10016

9 8 7 6 5 4 3 2 1

ISBN 1-55788-279-7

By arrangement with Salamander Books Ltd.

Home Economist: Oona van den Berg
Printed and bound in Spain by Bookprint, S.L.

CONTENTS

INTRODUCTION

Food fashions in the West keep looking further east for inspiration and now seem to have reached Japan.

Contrary to the general belief that Japanese food looks much too beautiful to eat and thus too complicated to cook, many dishes can be prepared very quickly, using almost no fat and very small amounts of fuel. This book shows you easy ways to cook authentic Japanese dishes, using ingredients that are readily available in supermarkets and Asian shops. You will see how easily you can adapt Japanese food to your daily cooking and bring true Japanese taste to your dinner table.

There are more than 80 recipes, including famous sushi, soups, fish, and shellfish, chicken and meat, vegetable side dishes, rice and noodles. Each recipe is illustrated in full color, with clear step-by-step instructions, to make Japanese cooking accessible to all.

JAPANESE FOOD

Japan was an agricultural nation for thousands of years until after the second world war. Houses were traditionally constructed mostly of wood, as opposed to Western houses made of stone, so wood was, and still is, a very valuable resource.

With few other fuel resources, the Japanese had to find various ways of appreciating both their agricultural produce and the plentiful supply of fish caught in the surrounding seas without burning lots of wood and charcoal. Consequently, the Japanese developed ways of eating raw or near raw food.

Eating totally raw fish may seem intimidating to the Western world but in Japan it is considered the best, if not the only, way to appreciate the real flavor of fish, and sashimi (prepared raw fish) has pride of place in a Japanese meal. Fish for sashimi must be really fresh – frozen fish cannot be used. It should be refrigerated until ready to use and handled as little as possible. To ensure freshness, Japanese restaurants often keep fish for sashimi alive in tanks until they are required.

Another Japanese speciality is sushi, based on boiled rice which is flavored with a rice vinegar mixture while warm. It is then fanned to cool it quickly and give it a glossy sheen. There is a wide variety of sushi, such as raw fish seasoned with wasabi (hot green horseradish) and layered with or wrapped around the rice, or sushi rolls made with vegetables or fish enclosed in sushi rice, wrapped in nori seaweed, then rolled up and sliced.

Due to Shintoism, the ancient mythological religion, and later Buddhism, which was introduced from China, the Japanese remained a non-carnivorous nation until the opening up of the country to Western influences towards the end of the nineteenth century.

Today, despite Japan's economic growth and the pressure from overseas governments to open up the domestic market, Japan is still largely a nation of fish and vegetable eaters. When meat is used, it is sliced thinly and normally cooked with vegetables. As a result, Japanese cooking is naturally healthy without even trying to be so.

COOKING AND SERVING

The most important part of Japanese cooking is the cutting of ingredients. The object is to cook vegetables of various shapes and textures to just the right crunchy softness so that they look very appetizing and taste as good as they look. Different cuts and shapes have their own names; for example:

Sengiri(shreds)
Wagiri (rounds)
Hangetsu (half-moons)
Tanzaku (literally, poem card – oblong and thin)
Hyoshigi (thick rectangles)
Sainome (cubes)
Arare (dice)
Sasagaki (shavings)
Hanagiri (flowers)

Cooking and Serving
Whether the food is being cooked for a formal banquet or a family meal, it is always very lightly done so that it is still crisp.

A formal Japanese banquet will start with hors d'oeuvres, clear soup and sashimi (prepared raw fish). This is followed in turn by a grilled dish, a steamed dish, a simmered dish and a deep-fried dish, all accompanied by vinegared or dressed salad, and the meal is finished with boiled rice, miso soup and pickles.

There are not many dessert dishes in Japanese cuisine, probably due to the fact that as sugar is used in so many savory dishes there is no need to supplement sugar intake. Another reason, of course, is that the vast amount of food eaten leaves little room for more by the end of the meal. Japanese cakes, which are eaten at tea time with green tea, are too sweet and heavy to eat after a meal, so fresh fruit and green tea almost always end a lengthy banquet. Warmed sake is drunk throughout the meal.

A simple traditional dinner at home will consist of soup and boiled rice with three main dishes – sashimi, a grilled dish and a simmered dish – all served at the same time.

JAPANESE UTENSILS

It is not necessary to buy any Japanese utensils if your kitchen is equipped with a good selection of Western cooking utensils, but the following items are particularly useful.

Daikon Grater

Japanese cooking uses a lot of grated daikon (mooli) and ginger root. An ordinary cheese grater would do the job but it is worth investing in a daikon grater which allows the juices from the ingredients to be captured in the curved base as they are grated.

Hashi

A pair of hashi (chopsticks) are the most useful tools for handling small pieces of food when cooking in the kitchen and they are the most elegant cutlery to eat with in the dining room. Although they are popularly known as chopsticks in the West – a nick-name that originally meant 'nimble sticks' – this name is confusing, as hashi are not meant to chop anything. In Japanese cooking, food is served in properly cut sizes, so that you and your guests do not need to do any cutting at the table.

Once you master the art of using hashi you will find even the long, thick cooking hashi much better than forks for picking up and turning bacon and sausages while they are cooking.

Knives

Because cutting is so important in Japanese cooking, naturally Japanese knives are the cook's most cherished utensils. A Japanese chef's personal set of knives are his heart and soul and they move with him. While you do not need to have a set of Japanese knives, it is essential to have a good carving knife and a vegetable knife.

Makisu

This is a piece of bamboo blind the size of a table mat which is used mainly for rolling sushi. You can roll sushi with any flexible place mat of a similar texture, but if you are planning to make rolled sushis on a regular basis it is worth buying an authentic makisu (rolling mat).

Molds

There are many shaped molds but rectangular and flower ones are the most popular and the most useful. A rectangular mold is used to make pressed sushis, such as mackerel or smoked salmon, and the flower shaped one is used for pretty pieces of sushis and hors d'oeuvres.

JAPANESE INGREDIENTS

Japanese cooking probably uses more varieties of both fresh and dried fish than any other country's cuisine and, fortunately, many of these are now to be found at good fishmongers and Japanese and Chinese supermarkets in the West. Due to the popularity of Chinese cooking, many Japanese vegetables are also available.

Daikon

This is a large, long white radish, also known as mooli, which is often grated and used to make sauces in Japanese cooking.

Dried Red Chile

Called 'hawk's claw' in Japan because of its shape. Twice as hot as fresh chile.

Ginger

Ginger root, peeled and grated, is very popular in Japanese cooking. Vinegared ginger is also used a great deal. It is available in packages.

Hakusai

More commonly known as Chinese cabbage but Japanese in origin, the good thing about this vegetable is that unlike other vegetables it keeps fresh for quite a long time in the refrigerator, making it a convenient standby in an emergency. It is particularly good for making pickles.

Konbu

This is a giant seaweed called kelp which is sold in dried form at Japanese supermarkets. Full of vitamins and minerals, it is a health food best eaten simmered with other vegetables. Also used for dashi (fish stock).

Konnyaku

A gel-like cake made from yam flour, it has no taste or nutritional value but is eaten for its texture. It is considered a good, healthy diet food as it cleans the stomach. It is available fresh in packages at Japanese supermarkets.

Mirin

This is a thick sweet rice wine which gives a very subtle sweet flavor to dishes. It is widely used at fashionable modern restaurants. If not available, sweet sherry can be substituted but reduce the amount of sugar in the dish to a half or a third.

Miso

Miso is a very salty paste made from fermented soybeans. It is used for soup and salad dressings and is also good in marinades for fish and meat. There are two basic types, an orangey-brown which is slightly sweeter and a reddish-brown one which is saltier.

Rice

Authentic Japanese rice, which is short-grain and slightly sticky, is kept for the home market. Californian short-grain or medium-grain is a good substitute and Spain also produces a Japanese-style rice. These rices vary in hardness, but Kaho-mai, Nishiki, Maruyu, Kokuho (Californian) and Minori (Spanish) – listed in order of hardness – are popular brand names.

Rice Vinegar

Japanese vinegar, made from rice, is a very mild vinegar. It is essential to use this for making sushi rice. You can buy it at Asian shops.

Sake

A strong rice wine which is made from fermented rice and water. Along with tea, it is Japan's most famous drink and the one most frequently served with meals, usually lukewarm.

Sansho pepper

A delicately pungent Japanese green pepper, which is not used for cooking but as a condiment at the table. It is available in bottles at Asian shops.

Shiitake Mushrooms

This is a widely used mushroom and is the best-known among the Japanese varieties in the West. They are also known as Chinese mushrooms. Larger supermarkets stock fresh shiitake nowadays and dried ones can be found at any Asian food shop. Dried ones have a stronger flavor than fresh.

Shoyu

The most important ingredient in Japanese cooking, known in the West as soy sauce though the Japanese name is shoyu. The word 'soy' is a regional dialect of southern Japan from where shoyu was first exported. Shoyu is made from soybeans, flour and water which is fermented and matured for several months.

Tofu

Also called bean curd, tofu is made from yellow soybeans and is widely used as a health food. In Japan tofu shops still make it every day and traditionally there are two kinds, silk or cotton, made from soy milk sieved through silk or cotton cloth.

You can buy fresh as well as pre-packed tofu. These are available in both silken and regular (cotton) forms. Firmness of texture varies from firm to soft, depending on use; the firm one is generally recommended for cooking. Reduced fat tofu is also available.

Wakame

Young brown seaweed with a delicate flavor and soft but crisp texture; it is normally available in cut and dried form. It is used for soups and salads.

Wasabi

Hot, green horseradish, sold in tubes or powdered form, and used with raw fish. Mix powdered wasabi with the same amount of warm water.

DASHI

4-inch square of dried konbu (kelp)
1½ oz. hana-katsuo (dried bonito flakes)

Wipe konbu with a damp cloth, place in a saucepan with 3 cups water and soak about 1 hour. Heat, uncovered, over medium heat about 10 minutes, removing the konbu just before reaching boiling point so it retains its subtle flavor. If the thickest part of the konbu is still hard, return it to the pan a few more minutes, adding a little water to prevent it boiling. Reserve the konbu.

Add 1 oz. of the hana-katsuo to the pan. Bring back to a boil (do not stir) and immediately remove from the heat. Using a tablespoon or ladle, remove the foam from surface and let stand a few minutes until the hana-katsuo settles down to the bottom of pan. Strain the liquid through a sieve lined with muslin and reserve the hana-katsuo. This dashi (known as first dashi) is good for clear soups; however, for strongly flavored soups, noodle broths and simmering, second dashi is used.

To make second dashi, put reserved konbu and hana-katsuo in a saucepan with 3 cups water and bring to a boil. Lower the heat and simmer, uncovered, 10 to 15 minutes until dashi is reduced by one third. Add the last ½ oz. hana-katsuo and remove from heat. Skim off the foam, let stand and strain as for first dashi.

Makes 4 servings.

Note: For instant dashi, mix dashi-no-moto (freeze-dried dashi powder) with water.

—CLEAR SOUP WITH CHICKEN—

3½ oz. chicken breast fillet
6 teaspoons cornstarch
12 snow peas
DASHI SOUP:
1 recipe Dashi, opposite
1 tablespoon shoyu
½ teaspoon salt

Slice chicken breast crosswise diagonally into 8 pieces and pat lightly with cornstarch.

Bring a saucepan of water to a boil and drop in the chicken pieces, one at a time, so that they do not stick together. Cook a few minutes (do not overcook), then drain in a mesh bowl or a colander. Keep them warm. Remove strings from the snow peas, trim ends and slice diagonally. Cook in boiling water 1 to 2 minutes until soft but still crunchy. Set aside.

Heat dashi and season with the shoyu and salt. Place 2 pieces of cooked chicken breast and 3 snow peas in each of 4 individual soup bowls. Pour hot soup over them and serve at once.

Makes 4 servings.

—CLEAR SOUP WITH SHRIMP—

4 raw jumbo shrimp or 8 medium-size shrimp
3 tablespoons sake or 6 tablespoons white wine
1½ oz. dried somen (very fine) noodles
Cress, to garnish
DASHI SOUP:
1 recipe Dashi, page 12
1 tablespoon shoyu
½ teaspoon salt

Make a slit lengthwise along the back of each shrimp and remove the black vein-like intestine.

Place shrimp in a saucepan with the sake and 3 tablespoons water, or with the white wine only, and steam 2 to 3 minutes. Remove from the heat and let cool in the saucepan. Peel the shrimp, leaving the tail shell on. Cook the noodles in boiling water about 3 minutes then rinse in cold water, changing the water several times. Divide the noodles among 4 individual soup bowls. Place one large shrimp or 2 medium-size ones on each portion of noodles.

Heat the dashi and season with the shoyu and salt. Pour the hot soup gently over the shrimp and noodles and garnish with a few sprigs of cress.

Makes 4 servings.

──MISO SOUP WITH TOFU──

2 tablespoons dried wakame (seaweed)
3 tablespoons miso
4 oz. firm tofu, cut into tiny dice
1 green onion, finely chopped
Ground sansho pepper (optional)
STOCK:
2 cups second Dashi, page 12, or 2½ cups water
 and 1to 2 teaspoons dashi no-moto (freeze-dried
 dashi powder)

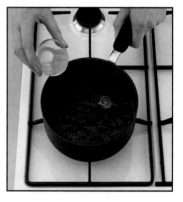

First make the second dashi, following the method on page 12, or add dashi no-moto to boiling water and stir to dissolve.

Lower heat and simmer 5 to 10 minutes, then remove from heat and strain through a muslin-lined sieve. Meanwhile, soak the wakame in plenty of water 10 to 15 minutes until fully opened up. Drain and cut the wakame into small pieces, if necessary.

Put the miso in a teacup and mix with a few spoonfuls of the stock. Return the stock to a low heat (do not boil) and add the diluted miso. Add the wakame and tofu to the pan and increase the heat. Just before it reaches the boiling point, add the finely chopped onion and immediately remove from the heat. Do not boil. Serve hot in individual soup bowls. Sprinkle with a little ground sansho pepper, if desired.

Makes 4 servings.

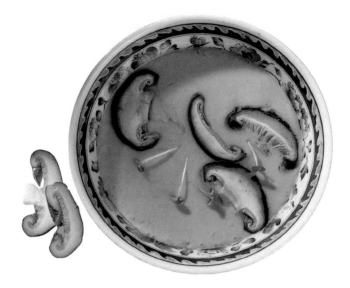

—EGG CUSTARD SOUP—

2½ to 3 oz. chicken breast, skinned
1 teaspoon each sake and shoyu
4 raw shrimp, peeled and deveined
4 fresh shiitake or button mushrooms
Cress, to garnish
STOCK:
2 cups dashi, page 12 or chicken
   stock
½ teaspoon salt
1 tablespoon mirin or ½ tablespoon sugar
1 tablespoon shoyu
3 eggs, beaten

Slice chicken diagonally into small pieces; sprinkle with sake and the 1 teaspoon shoyu.

Marinate the chicken 15 minutes, then drain. Parboil the shrimp 30 seconds and drain. Cut the stems off the mushrooms and quarter each one by slicing diagonally at the thickest part to make pieces with an even thickness. To make the stock, heat the dashi or chicken stock and season with the salt, mirin and 1 tablespoon shoyu. Allow to cool, then gradually pour into beaten eggs, stirring gently all the time. (The mixture should not form bubbles or foam.)

Divide the shrimp, chicken and mushrooms among 4 soup or tea cups and pour in egg soup until the cups are three quarters full. Cover the cups with foil. Place in a steamer and steam, covered, over low heat 25 to 30 minutes. Arrange a few sprigs of cress on top, leave covered 5 minutes, then serve hot.

Makes 4 servings.

Variation: Cook cups in oven in a shallow baking dish half-filled with hot water at 425F (220C) 25 minutes until set.

SUSHI RICE

2 cups short-grain rice
VINEGARY SUMESHI:
⅓ **cup rice vinegar**
1 tablespoon sugar
1 teaspoon salt

Wash the rice thoroughly, changing the water several times until it becomes clear.

Put the rice in a deep 5- to 6-inch saucepan, with 20 per cent more cold water than rice: to do this, first cover the rice with water, then add another ½-⅔ cup of water – the water should come about ⅔ inch above the rice. Leave 1 hour. Place the pan, covered, over high heat 5 minutes or until you hear a sizzling noise. Reduce heat and simmer gently 10 minutes, without lifting lid. Remove from heat and leave covered 10 minutes. To make the sumeshi, put vinegar, sugar and salt in a cup and mix until sugar and salt have dissolved.

Transfer rice to a large bowl and gradually fold in vinegar mixture, using a wooden spatula. Do not stir. Cool the rice to room temperature using a fan; this will make it shiny. It is now ready to make sushis.

Makes 4 servings.

Variation: To make a sweet sumeshi, add 1 tablespoon mirin to the rice cooking water. Mix ¼ cup rice vinegar, 1½ tablespoons sugar and ½ teaspoon salt. Fold into the cooked rice, as above.

MIXED SUSHI

3 to 4 dried shiitake mushrooms
1½ tablespoons sugar
3½ tablespoons shoyu
½ carrot, peeled and shredded
1 to 1½ cups Dashi, page 12
3 tablespoons sake
3½ oz. crab sticks, shredded
1 oz. green beans, trimmed
Vegetable oil for frying
1 egg, beaten with a pinch of salt
SUSHI RICE:
3½ cups short-grain rice
2 tablespoons mirin
½ cup rice vinegar
2½ tablespoons sugar
¾ teaspoon salt

Soak the rice as for sushi rice, see page 17. Meanwhile, soak the shiitake mushrooms in warm water 30 minutes, then drain, reserving ⅓ cup of the water. Discard stems and cut caps into thin strips. Put reserved soaking water in a pan with the sugar, 1½ tablespoons shoyu and mushroom caps and cook 20 minutes or until almost all liquid is absorbed. Parboil carrot and cook in seasoned with 2 tablespoons each shoyu and sake 3 to 4 minutes. Sprinkle remaining sake over the crab sticks. Lightly cook beans and slice diagonally.

Add a pinch of salt to the egg and stir well. Heat a frying pan, pour in some vegetable oil, then remove from heat and wipe off excess oil. Return to medium heat and pour in egg so that a paper-thin layer covers the entire surface. Break air bubbles and fry both sides 30 seconds. Turn onto a board, leave to cool, then cut into shreds. Make sushi rice, see page 17; while warm, fold in mushrooms, carrots and crab sticks. Garnish with beans and egg shreds.

Makes 4 to 6 servings.

SUSHI IN PANCAKE PACKAGES

1 to 2 dried shiitake mushrooms
3½ oz. dried shrimp
3 tablespoons sake or white wine
2 tablespoons each shoyu
4½ tablespoons sugar
1 sheet of nori (wafer-thin dried seaweed)
2 teaspoons sesame seeds
6 teaspoons cornstarch
8 eggs, beaten
Vegetable oil for frying
12 to 16 sprigs watercress
SUSHI RICE:
1 cup short-grain rice
1 tablespoon mirin
¼ cup rice vinegar
1½ tablespoons sugar and ½ teaspoon salt

Soak the rice for sushi rice, see page 17. Soak mushrooms in warm water and shrimp in sake or wine 30 minutes. Drain the mushrooms, reserving ⅓ cup of the water. Put the reserved water in a pan with the shoyu and 2 tablespoons sugar, add the mushrooms and cook 10 minutes. Leave to cool, then finely chop. Meanwhile, drain the shrimp and chop roughly if large. Place nori over heat and lightly grill both sides for a second until crisp. Crumble it in paper towels. In a dry saucepan, toast sesame seeds and crush roughly.

Mix cornstarch with 2 tablespoons water and stir into eggs with remaining 2½ tablespoons sugar. Heat a crepe pan and wipe a little oil over bottom. Add a little of the eggs, tilting pan to spread evenly. Cook 1 minute on each side. Repeat to make 12 to 16 very thin pancakes. Make sushi rice, and, while warm, fold in nori, shrimp, mushrooms and sesame seeds. Wrap 2 to 3 tablespoonfuls of rice in a pancake, then tie up like a money bag with watercress.

Makes 12 to 16.

MACKEREL SUSHI

1 lb. 2 oz. mackerel, filleted
Salt and rice vinegar
SUSHI RICE:
1 cup short-grain rice
2½ tablespoons rice vinegar
½ tablespoon sugar
½ teaspoon salt
GARNISH:
Lemon wedges and cress
Vinegared ginger slices, optional

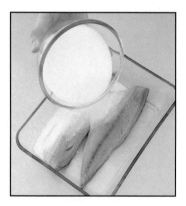

Start the preparation for this dish 1 to 2 days beforehand. Place the mackerel fillets in a dish, cover completely with plenty of salt and leave overnight in the refrigerator.

Make the sushi rice, see page 17. Remove mackerel and rub off the salt with paper towels. Carefully remove all the bones with tweezers. Wash off any remaining salt with rice vinegar. Using your fingers, remove transparent skin from each fillet, leaving silver pattern on flesh intact. Place a fillet, skinned side down, in a wet wooden mold or rectangular container, about 10 x 3 x 2 inches, lined with a large piece of plastic wrap. Fill the gaps with small pieces taken from the other fillet so the mold is lined.

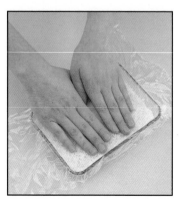

Press sushi rice down firmly on top of the fish with fingers. Put the wet wooden lid on, or fold in the plastic wrap, and place a weight on top. Refrigerate 2 to 3 hours or overnight. Remove from container, unwrap, and cut into small pieces with a sharp knife, wiping the knife with a vinegar-soaked cloth or paper after each cut. Garnish with lemon, cress, and vinegared ginger slices, if desired. Serve with shoyu handed separately in small individual dishes.

Makes 4 to 6 servings as a starter.

——SMOKED SALMON SUSHI——

2 tablespoons Dashi, page 12
2 tablespoons shoyu
6 oz. smoked salmon, thickly sliced
Capers and lemon wedges, to garnish
SUSHI RICE:
1 cup short-grain rice
2½ tablespoons rice vinegar
½ tablespoon sugar
½ teaspoon salt

Make the sushi rice, see page 17. Mix the dashi and shoyu, sprinkle it over the smoked salmon and marinate for at least 30 minutes. Drain well and pat dry.

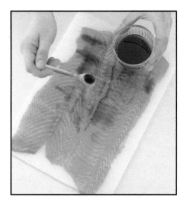

Lay half the salmon evenly in bottom of a wet wooden mold or rectangular container, measuring 10 x 3 x 2 inches, lined with a large piece of plastic wrap. Using hands, firmly press down enough sushi rice to make a ½-inch layer on top. Repeat this with the rest of the smoked salmon and rice to make a 1¼-inch-thick, double-layer sushi. Put wet wooden lid on, or fold in plastic wrap, and place a weight on top. Refrigerate 2 to 3 hours or overnight.

Remove from container, unwrap, and cut into bite-size pieces, using a sharp knife to prevent the layers separating, and wiping the knife with a vinegar-soaked cloth or paper after each cut. Arrange pieces on a Japanese lacquered tray, or a large serving plate, and garnish with some capers on top and lemon wedges by the side. Serve on individual plates with a little shoyu.

Makes 4 to 6 servings as a starter.

──CHERRY BLOSSOM SUSHI──

⅓ teaspoon salt
2 teaspoons sake
3 tablespoons cooked peeled small shrimp
2 teaspoons sesame seeds
3½ oz. cod fillet
2 tablespoons sugar
Red vegetable food coloring
Watercress sprigs, to garnish
SUSHI RICE:
1 cup short-grain rice
1 tablespoon mirin
¼ cup rice vinegar
1½ tablespoons sugar
½ teaspoon salt

Soak rice as for sushi rice, see page 17. Meanwhile, sprinkle a pinch of salt and a dash of sake over the shrimp. Heat a small dry saucepan and toast the sesame seeds, then put them in a mortar and crush 2 to 3 times with a pestle just to bring out the flavor. Make the sushi rice, see page 17, and, while still warm, fold in the shrimp and sesame seeds. Cook the cod fillet in just enough boiling water to cover, then drain. Skin the fillet, carefully remove all the small bones and pat dry with paper towels.

Using a fork, crush fish to make fine flakes. Put fish, sugar and remaining sake and salt in a pan and cook over low heat 1 minute, stirring. Dilute a drop of food coloring agent with a little water and add to pan, stirring vigorously to spread the color evenly. Lay some pink flakes on bottom of a small flower mold and press some rice on top. Turn out on to a plate. Repeat until all the fish and rice are used. Arrange as 'cherry blossoms' on serving plates with watercress for leaves.

Makes 4 to 6 servings as a starter.

NORI-ROLLED SUSHI

2½-inch piece cucumber
Wasabi paste or powder
3 sheets of nori (wafer-thin dried seaweed)
3½ oz. fresh tuna or smoked salmon, cut into ¼-inch strips
2½-inch takuan (pickled daikon), cut into ¼-inch strips
Vinegared ginger slices, to garnish
SUSHI RICE:
1 cup short-grain rice
¼ cup rice vinegar
1 tablespoon sugar and 1 teaspoon salt

Make the sushi rice, see page 17, and set aside.

Quarter cucumber lengthwise, discarding the seed part, and cut into ¼-inch-thick strips. If using wasabi powder, dissolve about 1 teaspoon in the same amount of water in a small cup and stir well to make a soft, but not runny, clay-like texture. Set aside with the cup upside down (to prevent air getting into it). Halve the nori sheets. Place one at a time horizontally on a makisu (rolling mat). Using your hands, spread about 2 to 3 tablespoons of the rice on it, leaving about ½-inch margin on the side furthest from you.

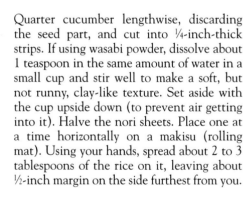

Spread a tiny amount of wasabi paste across the rice in the center and place a row of half the cucumber strips on it. Roll up the mat from side nearest you, wrapping cucumber in the center. Repeat to make another roll with remaining cucumber, then make 2 rolls using tuna or salmon, and 2 using the takuan, omitting wasabi in takuan rolls. Trim ends of rolls and cut each one into 6 pieces. Arrange on a serving plate, garnish with ginger and serve with a little shoyu on individual plates.

───THICK ROLLED SUSHI───

2 extra-large eggs, beaten
2 tablespoons Dashi, page 12
2 teaspoons sake and ⅓ teaspoon salt
5 tablespoons sugar
4 to 5 dried shiitake mushrooms
2 tablespoons shoyu
5 oz. cod fillet
Red food coloring
⅓ cucumber, shredded
4 sheets of nori (wafer-thin dried seaweed)
SUSHI RICE:
2½ cups short-grain rice
¼ cup rice vinegar
2⅓ teaspoons sugar
⅓ teaspoon salt

Make sushi rice, see page 17, and set aside. In a small pan, make a firm omelet using the eggs mixed with the dashi, sake, salt and 2½ tablespoons sugar, see page 26, and cut into ¼-inch-thick strips. Soak the dried shiitake mushrooms in warm water 30 minutes, then drain, reserving ⅓ cup of soaking water. Trim stems off and cut mushroom caps into thin strips. Place in a pan with reserved soaking water, shoyu and remaining sugar; cook 10 minutes. Cook the cod and make pink cod flakes, see Cherry Blossom Sushi, page 22.

Place one nori sheet vertically on a makisu (rolling mat). Spread ¼ of the rice evenly over it, leaving ¾-inch margin at furthest side. Put one strip each of all the ingredients across center of rice and roll up from side nearest you. Keeping end of the nori down, press firmly into a round shape. Repeat to make 3 more rolls. Let settle at least 30 minutes, then cut each roll into 6. Arrange on a serving plate and serve with a little shoyu in individual dishes.

Makes 24 pieces.

─────── HAND-ROLLED SUSHI ───────

3½ cups short-grain rice
4 to 5 dried shiitake mushrooms
2½ tablespoons sugar
1 tablespoon mirin
2 tablespoons shoyu, plus extra for dipping
8 oz. fresh tuna
4 oz. smoked salmon
8 raw jumbo shrimp
1 avocado
⅓ cucumber, shredded
1 package of cress
8 sheets of nori (wafer-thin dried seaweed)

Soak the short-grain rice as for sushi rice, see page 17.

Meanwhile, soak the shiitake mushrooms in warm water 30 minutes, then drain, reserving ⅓ cup soaking water. Trim stems off and cut mushroom caps into thin strips. Place in a pan with the sugar, mirin, 2 tablespoons shoyu and the reserved soaking water; cook for 10 minutes. Slice the tuna into 2 x 1-inch thin pieces. Cut the smoked salmon into similar-size slices. Peel, devein and lightly boil the shrimp. Drain and slice horizontally in half. Peel, pit and thinly slice the avocado.

Boil rice, see page 17, and divide between 4 individual serving bowls with lids to keep rice warm. On a large serving plate, arrange all the prepared ingredients and place it in the center of the table. Lightly grill both sides of nori sheets over low heat and cut each one into 4 squares so that each diner has 8 small sheets. At the table, take one sheet in your palm, put in a little boiled rice, spreading it with a spatula or fork. Wrap some ingredients in it, dip in shoyu and eat.

Makes 4 servings.

─────ROLLED OMELET─────

½ cup warm Dashi, page 12, or chicken stock
⅓ teaspoon salt
2 teaspoons mirin or 1 teaspoon sugar
⅔ tablespoon shoyu, plus extra for serving
6 eggs, lightly beaten
Vegetable oil for frying
Grated daikon (mooli), to garnish

Mix the warm stock, salt, mirin or sugar, and shoyu in a bowl and gently stir in the beaten eggs. Place a large frying pan over medium heat and wipe bottom with vegetable oil, using a cloth or paper towels.

When the pan is just hot, pour one-third of the mixture into the pan and tilt to spread it evenly over bottom. Break the air bubbles with a fork. When the egg is nearly firm, fold about 1 inch from left and right sides in towards the center to make an oblong shape then, with chopsticks or spatula, roll the egg layer towards you. Using the oily cloth or paper towel, oil the empty part of the pan, push the just-rolled egg to the other side and complete the oiling of the bottom. Keeping the egg roll at the other end, pour half of the remaining mixture into the pan.

Tilt pan to spread mixture evenly and allow it to run beneath egg roll. When the second layer starts to set, repeat the rolling, using the first roll as the core. Without removing the roll from the pan, repeat once more with remaining egg. Turn out onto a makisu (rolling mat) and wrap tightly. Some juice should run out if omelet is not overdone. Leave to settle for a few minutes, then unwrap and cut into 4. Serve on individual plates, garnished with daikon and shoyu.

Makes 4 servings.

EGG TOFU

2½ cups Dashi, page 12, or chicken stock
1 tablespoon salt
3 tablespoons each mirin and shoyu
6 eggs, well beaten but not frothy
Finely sliced peel from ½ lemon, to garnish
Hana-katsuo (dried bonito flakes), to serve
SAUCE:
1 cup Dashi
3 tablespoons mirin
3 tablespoons shoyu

Line the bottom and 2 of the sides of an 8-inch square baking dish with a sheet of foil, allowing excess foil to hang over the sides.

In a bowl, mix the dashi or chicken stock, salt, mirin and shoyu and stir in beaten eggs. Pour the mixture into the lined dish and steam in a steamer 3 minutes. Reduce the heat to low and continue steaming 25 minutes. Remove dish from the steamer and run a knife along the unlined sides. Lift out egg tofu, holding the 2 hanging ends of the foil, and place it on a cutting board.

Cut egg tofu into 8 cakes and place 2 cakes in each of 4 deep individual dishes. In a saucepan, mix the sauce ingredients and bring to a boil. Remove from heat and gently pour sauce over the egg tofu cakes. Arrange sliced lemon peel and hana-katsuo on top and serve. To serve cold, chill the tofu and sauce separately.

Makes 4 servings.

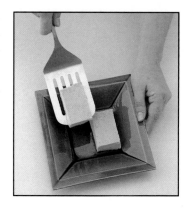

—FRIED TOFU IN DASHI SAUCE—

4-inch piece large daikon (mooli), peeled
1 dried or fresh red chile, seeded
2 cakes firm tofu
All-purpose flour for coating
Vegetable oil for deep-frying
SAUCE:
1 cup Dashi, page 12
2½ tablespoons shoyu
2 tablespoons mirin

Poke a chopstick into the daikon to make a few holes lengthwise. Push in dried chile strips; if using a fresh chile, make one large hole in center of daikon by pushing in a peeler. Grate to make rust-colored daikon.

Combine sauce ingredients in a saucepan, heat and keep warm. Quarter each tofu cake, roll in the flour and pat off excess. Heat the oil in a deep-fat fryer to 350F (180C) and fry the tofu pieces, 4 at a time, about 8 minutes or until lightly golden, turning 2 to 3 times. Remove from the oil and drain on paper towels.

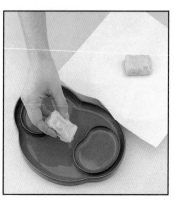

Arrange the fried tofu pieces, 2 at a time in individual dishes, on decorative paper napkins if desired. Serve warm sauce in a gravy boat and the daikon relish in a bowl so that diners can mix the two to make their own sauce. Serve accompanied by small dishes for the dipping sauce.

Makes 4 servings.

Note: The rust-colored grated daikon, known as momiji-orishi (autumn maple leaf relish), is best grated with a daikon grater.

-FRIED TOFU WITH VEGETABLES-

2 cakes tofu
Vegetable oil for deep-frying
10 Chinese cabbage leaves (hakusai)
3½ oz. spinach
1 cup Dashi, page 12
2 tablespoons shoyu
1 tablespoon sugar

Parboil tofu 3 to 5 minutes, drain and pat dry. Heat oil in a frying pan over high heat and add tofu cakes, one at a time. Deep-fry a few minutes or until golden brown all over, turning 2 to 3 times. Remove from pan, drain and cool on paper towels.

Parboil cabbage leaves for a few minutes and cut into 2-inch strips. Roughly chop the spinach. Halve deep-fried tofu lengthwise and then cut into ¼-inch-thick slices. Heat the dashi over medium heat and add the cabbage, shoyu and sugar. Stir well, then add the spinach and fried tofu slices. Simmer 1 to 2 minutes. Check the seasoning, then remove from heat.

In 4 deep individual dishes, arrange some cabbage, then put spinach and fried tofu on top and pour over the simmering soup. Serve immediately.

Makes 4 servings.

GRILLED TOFU WITH MISO SAUCE

2 cakes firm tofu
Toasted sesame seeds for sprinkling
Bamboo leaves, to garnish
MISO SAUCE:
3½ oz. miso
1 egg yolk
1 tablespoon each sake, mirin and sugar
4 tablespoons Dashi, page 12
Juice of ¼ lime

Wrap each tofu cake in a cloth and place a light weight, such as a plate, on top to squeeze out the water. Let stand at least 1 hour.

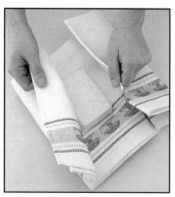

To make sauce, put the miso in a bowl and blend in the egg yolk, sake, mirin and sugar. Place bowl over a saucepan of simmering water. Gradually add the dashi and cook, stirring, until sauce becomes thick but not too hard, then add the lime juice. Remove from the heat immediately and cool to room temperature (it will keep well in the refrigerator, if desired.)

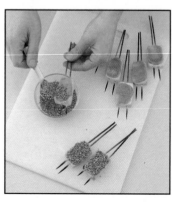

Preheat broiler. Unwrap the tofu cakes and cut into 2 x ¾ x ½-inch slices. Skewer each of the slices lengthwise with 2 bamboo skewers. Broil them under high heat a few minutes on each side until lightly browned and heated through. Remove from heat and, using a small spatula, thickly spread one side with miso sauce. Sprinkle with the toasted sesame seeds. Grill miso-covered side 1 to 2 minutes. Repeat on the other side. Serve hot on skewers on a bed of bamboo leaves.

Makes 4 servings as a starter.

CUCUMBER IN VINEGAR DRESSING

2 packages cut dried wakame
1 cucumber
1 teapoon salt
Ginger root, peeled and shredded, to garnish only
VINEGAR DRESSING:
4 tablespoons rice vinegar
1 tablespoon shoyu
½ tablespoon sugar

Soak the wakame in tepid water 5 to 15 minutes, or according to package instructions, until fully expanded. Halve the cucumber lengthwise and, using a tablespoon, roughly scoop out seeds.

Slice cucumber halves very thinly to make half-moons and spread out on a cutting board. Sprinkle them with the salt and mash with your hand a few times. Using both hands, squeeze out the water, then put cucumber in a medium bowl. Do not rinse. Drain the wakame and plunge in boiling water 1 minute. Drain and place under cold running water to cool down. Trim off any hard parts, then chop into bite-size pieces. Pat dry with paper towels and put in the bowl with cucumber.

Mix the vinegar, shoyu and sugar, stirring well until the sugar has dissolved. Pour over cucumber mixture and gently mix to fold the dressing into the cucumber and wakame. Arrange in a heap in the center of a shallow dish or in a salad bowl. Garnish with finely shredded ginger and serve.

Makes 4 servings.

—CHINESE CABBAGE & CHILES—

20 Chinese cabbage leaves (hakusai)
1 to 2 fresh red or green chiles, seeded
2 teaspoons salt
**2 tablespoons kimchee dressing (Korean chile and
    garlic dressing)**
Finely shredded lemon peel, to garnish

Wash and trim the Chinese cabbage leaves.
Cut in half lengthwise, then crosswise into 2
-inch pieces. Chop the chile into fine half-
rings.

Put ¼ of the Chinese leaves in a freezer bag
and sprinkle with ¼ of the salt and chile.
Add another ¼ of the leaves on top and
sprinkle with another ¼ of the salt and chile.
Repeat this two more times with the
remaining ingredients and shake the bag to
spread the salt and chile pieces evenly
throughout the leaves. Tie the bag almost
airtight and leave in the refrigerator at least
1 to 2 days, preferably 5 to 6 days.

Keeping leaves in the bag, squeeze out the
water, then turn out cabbage into a medium
bowl. Add kimchee dressing, mix well and
arrange on a serving dish. Garnish with the
shredded lemon peel and serve at once.

Makes 4 to 8 servings.

Note: Kimchee dressing is available in jars
at Asian shops, or use a spicy oil and vinegar
dressing.

——RADISH CHERRY BLOSSOM——

7 oz. red radishes
4 small turnips, peeled
1 teaspoon salt
1 cup rice vinegar
⅔ cup sugar
Watercress and pomegranate seeds, to garnish

Cut the stem part off the radishes and trim the turnips so that each will stand upright. Lay a pair of cheap chopsticks, or pencils, sideways in parallel on a cutting board and place a radish in between.

Using a sharp knife, carefully make 4 to 6 cuts down each radish until the blade touches the chopsticks or pencils, so that the radish is not cut quite through. Turn the radish 90 degrees and make a few more cuts across the cuts already made. Repeat this with all the remaining radishes and also with the turnips which need far more cuts because of the size. Divide the turnips into 4 to 6 wedges. Put all together in a large bowl, sprinkle with the salt and lightly rub in. Cover with a small plate, place a weight on plate and leave for 30 minutes.

Mix rice vinegar and sugar, stirring until the sugar has dissolved. Drain vegetables and pour the sauce over them. Let marinate overnight. The red color of the radishes will melt into sauce and make turnips cherry pink as well as the radishes. Divide the pink 'cherry blossoms' between 4 individual black lacquer trays or large plates. Arrange turnips as 'petals,' and watercress as 'leaves on twigs' around the 'flowers.' Arrange pomegranate seeds to look like 'fallen petals' underneath.

Makes 4 servings.

NAMASU SALAD

6-inch piece daikon (mooli), peeled
1 to 2 carrots
1 teaspoon salt
⅓ cup rice vinegar
3 tablespoons sugar
Finely shredded lime peel, to garnish

Cut the daikon and the carrots into three 2-inch pieces and slice each piece very thinly lengthwise and then shred into big matchsticks.

Place the matchsticks in a medium bowl and sprinkle them with the salt. Using your hand, gently mash them, then leave 15 to 20 minutes. Lightly squeeze out the water between your hands (do not press too hard) and put in another bowl.

Mix rice vinegar and sugar and stir well until the sugar has dissolved. Pour the mixture into daikon and carrot shreds and gently fold in to mix the 2 colors evenly. Heap mixture on a serving dish and garnish with lime peel. The Japanese regard the combination of red and white as celebration colors, so this dish is considered essential for a New Year's Day brunch table.

Makes 4 servings.

──FRENCH BEANS KINPIRA──

8 oz. green beans, trimmed, or 3 carrots or parsnips,
  peeled
1 dried or fresh red chile
2 tablespoons vegetable oil
2 tablespoons sake
2 tablespoons shoyu
1 tablespoon sugar

Cut the green beans diagonally into thin
strips. If using carrots or parsnips, cut them
into 2-inch pieces, slicing lengthwise and
then cut into strips.

If using dried chile, soak it in warm water 10
to 15 minutes until outer skin is softened. To
remove fresh or dried chile, cut it lengthwise
and scrape out the seeds with the back of the
knife blade. Chop the chile very finely.

Heat a wok or a large frying pan, add the oil
and tilt the pan to spread it over the bottom.
Stir in the chile and green bean, carrot or
parsnip strips and stir-fry over high heat
about 3 minutes until the vegetable strips
begin to soften. Lower heat and sprinkle
with the sake, shoyu and sugar. Stir-fry over
medium heat until the liquid is almost completely absorbed. Serve hot or at room temperature in one deep serving dish or in small,
deep individual dishes.

Makes 4 servings.

—SPINACH & SESAME DRESSING—

1 package fresh spinach, stemmed, or 7 oz. green beans, trimmed
SESAME (GOMA-AE) DRESSING:
5 tablespoons white sesame seeds
1½ teaspoons sugar
3 teaspoons shoyu
3 tablespoons Dashi, page 12

Prepare the dressing first. Heat a small dry saucepan and toast the sesame seeds.

Remove from the heat and transfer the seeds to a large suribachi (Japanese grinding bowl) or mortar. Crush and grind the seeds with a pestle until they form a paste. Add the sugar, shoyu and dashi to the mortar and blend vigorously to make a fairly smooth dressing.

Cook the spinach in lightly salted boiling water about 1 minute, then drain and immediately rinse under cold running water to cool it quickly and preserve the bright green color. Lightly squeeze out the water and chop roughly into 1¼-inch pieces. (If using green beans, cook them a few minutes until tender, then cut diagonally into thin strips.) Add the dressing to the spinach or beans, and gently fold in. Serve heaped in small deep dishes.

Makes 4 servings.

—TRICOLOR SALAD & SHOYU—

1 carrot
3½-in. piece large daikon (mooli), peeled
salt
5 oz. snow peas, trimmed
DRESSING:
1 tablespoon shoyu
3 tablespoons vegetable oil
2 tablespoons rice vinegar
⅓ teaspoon salt
Freshly ground black pepper

Chop the carrot and daikon separately into 1½-inch shreds. Put them in 2 large bowls and sprinkle each with a pinch of salt. Leave 15 minutes.

Cook the snow peas in boiling salted water 1 to 2 minutes until tender but still crisp. Drain and immediately rinse under cold running water. Slice each snow pea slightly diagonally into 3 pieces. Arrange the different vegetable shreds on a serving dish, each occupying one-third of the dish.

In a bowl, mix the shoyu, oil and vinegar. Add the salt and a pinch of pepper. Blend vigorously with a whisk and pour into a serving bowl or a gravy boat. The vegetables and the dressing are served separately and mixed together at the table before eating.

Makes 4 servings.

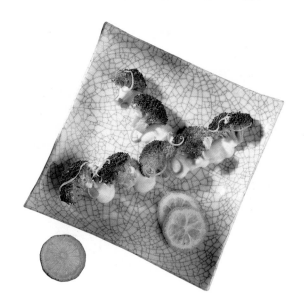

-BROCCOLI WITH MAYONNAISE-

2 lbs. broccoli, trimmed
DRESSING:
½ lemon
6 tablespoons mayonnaise
Juice of 1 lime

First make the dressing. Cut 2 to 3 thin slices from the lemon half and finely shred the peel from remainder. Put the mayonnaise in a small bowl and stir in the lime juice and half of the shredded lemon peel.

Make a cross slit on the bottom of the remaining stems of the broccoli so that the stems will cook as quickly as the green parts. Put the broccoli, head down, in a deep saucepan of salted boiling water and boil gently 2 to 3 minutes, turning a few times. Drain and separate into small sections.

Arrange the broccoli on a serving dish or individual plates and pour the mayonnaise over it. Sprinkle the remaining lemon peel on top and garnish with lemon slices. Serve at once.

Makes 4 servings.

Note: Lemon peel is preferable to lime peel in this dish because of the color as well as the flavor.

GRILLED EGGPLANT

4 eggplants, ends removed
Vegetable oil for frying
GINGER SAUCE:
⅓ cup Dashi, page 12
2 tablespoons shoyu
2 tablespoons mirin or 2 teaspoons sugar
2 tablespoons sake
1½-2 inch piece ginger root, peeled
8 fresh mint leaves
SESAME SAUCE:
3 tablespoons white sesame seeds
3 tablespoons Dashi
1½ tablespoons shoyu
½ tablespoon sugar
Salt

Make ginger sauce: put the dashi, shoyu, mirin or sugar and sake in a saucepan and boil 1 minute. Remove from heat and set aside. Grate ginger with a Japanese daikon grater or a cheese grater. Finely shred mint leaves. Make sesame sauce: toast sesame seeds in a small dry saucepan, then grind them to a paste in a suribachi (Japanese grinding bowl) or a mortar. Mix in the dashi and shoyu. Season with sugar and a pinch of salt. Slice eggplants lengthwise into quarters and fry, in batches, in a little oil over high heat 1 to 2 minutes on each side.

Place 2 eggplant pieces on each of 8 small plates. Arrange the grated ginger and mint slices on top of 4 of the plates and add the sauce. Pour the sesame sauce over the eggplant pieces on the other 4 plates. Serve one of each type to each person.

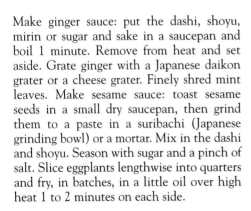

Makes 4 servings.

Note: This dish is also excellent cooked on a grill.

—VEGETABLE TEMPURA—

1 carrot
1 turnip or parsnip
7 oz. green beans, trimmed
Vegetable oil for deep-frying
½ daikon (mooli), peeled and grated
1½ to 2 inch piece ginger root, peeled and grated
Lemon wedges, to garnish
BATTER:
1 egg yolk
1 cup ice cold water
1 cup all-purpose flour, sifted
SAUCE:
1 cup Dashi, page 12
⅓ cup each shoyu and mirin

Cut carrot and turnip or parsnip into 2-inch long shreds. Cut beans diagonally into fine strips. Heat plenty of oil in a wok or deep-fryer to 340F (170C). Meanwhile, make the batter. In a large bowl, lightly beat the egg yolk and pour in the ice cold water. Stir just 2 to 3 times, then add the flour. Using 3 or 4 chopsticks or a fork, very lightly mix the batter with just a few strokes. Do not whisk or overmix – the batter should be very lumpy. Put all the vegetable shreds into the bowl and gently fold in.

Carefully drop a tablespoonful of battered vegetables at a time into the oil. Fry a few at a time and remove from the oil when both sides are light golden and drain on paper towels. Repeat until all the battered vegetables are cooked. Arrange them on a large serving platter or individual plates with heaps of grated daikon and ginger. Garnish with lemon wedges. Quickly heat the dashi, shoyu and mirin in a pan and pour it into small individual bowls. Serve hot.

Makes 4 servings.

CRAB STICK DAIKON ROLL

1 large daikon (mooli), peeled
4-inch square of dried konbu (kelp)
7 oz. crab sticks
1½-inch piece ginger root, peeled and cut into
    matchsticks
Watercress, to garnish
DRESSING:
2 dried or fresh red chiles
8 tablespoons Dashi, page 12
4 tablespoons rice vinegar
3 tablespoons sugar
Salt and 2 to 3 teaspoons vegetable oil

Slice daikon into ¹⁄₁₀-inch rounds and spread out on a wire rack. Dry 24 hours.

The next day, soak the konbu in warm water 10 minutes, then cut it lengthwise into ⅛-inch strips. Divide each crab stick lengthwise into 2 to 3 pieces. Place a piece of crab stick and 1 to 2 shreds of ginger on a dried and softened piece of daikon and roll up. Tie with a strip of konbu so that it won't open up. Repeat with remaining ingredients. Put all the rolls in a mesh bowl or colander and pour boiling hot water over rolls. Drain and set aside.

If using dried chiles, soak in warm water 10 minutes. Whether using dried or fresh, cut in half lengthwise and remove the seeds, then slice diagonally into thin strips. Put the dashi, rice vinegar, sugar, a little salt and oil in a saucepan and bring to a boil. Stir to dissolve sugar and add chile strips. Boil a few seconds and remove from heat. Leave to cool. Place daikon rolls in a bowl, pour over dressing and marinate overnight. Transfer to a serving dish and garnish with watercress.

Makes 4 to 8 servings as an hors d'oeuvre.

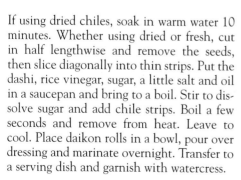

—BABY CLAMS WITH MUSTARD—

1 package fresh spinach, trimmed
A little shoyu
1 (10-oz.) can baby clams
Sake or white wine and salt
DRESSING:
1 teaspoon prepared mustard
2 tablespoons shoyu
1 tablespoon sake or white wine
1 tablespoon rice vinegar
⅓ teaspoon salt

Cook the spinach in salted boiling water 1 to 2 minutes and drain. Lightly squeeze the water out with your hands and cut the spinach into 2-inch long pieces.

Put the spinach in a bowl, sprinkle with a little shoyu and set aside. Drain the baby clams and pour boiling water over them. Drain well and sprinkle with a dash of sake or wine and salt. To make dressing, mix the mustard, shoyu, sake or wine, rice vinegar and salt. Stir well until the mustard has dissolved, then transfer the dressing to a small serving bowl or a ramekin.

Arrange the baby clams on a bed of spinach on a serving plate. Serve with the dressing on the side.

Makes 4 servings as a starter.

—SQUID & CUCUMBER SALAD—

1 lb. 2 oz. squid, cleaned
½ cucumber
Salt
DRESSING:
1 teaspoon prepared mustard
2 tablespoons shoyu
1 teaspoon sake
1 teaspoon sesame oil

Peel the outer skin off the squid, then cut squid in half lengthwise. Wash inside well and parboil, with the tentacles, 1 minute. Drain and immediately rinse under cold running water to stop further cooking.

Cut the body parts in half lengthwise and then crosswise into ¼-inch strips. Separate the tentacles and chop each into 1½-2-inch pieces. Put the squid in a large bowl.

Halve the cucumber lengthwise. Using a tablespoon, scoop out the seeds. Slice the cucumber into thin half-moons and sprinkle with a pinch of salt. Lightly mash with your hand to squeeze out the water, then add to the squid in the bowl. In a small cup, mix all the ingredients for the dressing and pour over the squid and cucumber mixture. Toss the squid and cucumber in the dressing and serve in small individual dishes.

Makes 4 servings as a starter.

–SASHIMI WITH WASABI SAUCE–

1 small octopus and salt
1½ lb. very fresh Dover or lemon sole, filleted
Lemon wedges and cress, to garnish
WASABI SAUCE:
Juice of ½ lemon
1½ tablespoons shoyu
½ tablespoon olive oil
1½ teaspoons wasabi paste or powder

Separate the octopus tentacles and clean, using a brush. Put in lightly salted boiling water and cook over medium heat 5 to 6 minutes. Drain and let cool slowly.

Carefully remove all the small bones from the sole. If filleted into 2 fillets, halve both lengthwise. Place a quartered sole fillet on a cutting board with the skin side down and insert the blade between the skin and the flesh at the tail-end. Firmly holding the tail end, run the blade carefully along the skin towards the head end to separate the flesh. Repeat with remaining fillets and slice crosswise into ⅔-inch-wide pieces, inserting the blade diagonally in line with the pattern of the fish flesh.

Chill octopus in the refrigerator, then slice tentacles and body into ¼-inch-thick rings, cutting diagonally. Mix all the sauce ingredients with 1 tablespoon water (if using powdered wasabi, mix it with a little warm water to form a paste before mixing with remaining sauce ingredients.) Arrange sole around edge of a large serving plate and heap octopus in center. Pour over half the sauce. Garnish with lemon and cress and serve accompanied by the rest of the sauce.

Makes 4 to 8 servings as an hors d'oeuvre.

──────SEA BASS HAKATA-OSHI──────

1 lb. 2 oz. very fresh sea bass, filleted and skinned
Salt
½ cup rice vinegar
½ cucumber
1½-inch piece ginger root
2 to 3 basil leaves, chopped
Lime slices, to garnish
VINEGAR DRESSING:
4 tablespoons each rice vinegar and Dashi, page 12
2 tablespoons shoyu
½ tablespoon sugar

Remove all small bones from fish and slice horizontally into ½-inch-thick slices.

Sprinkle fish with a pinch of salt and leave 5 minutes. Pat dry and marinate in the rice vinegar a few minutes. Meanwhile, slice the cucumber very thinly lengthwise and soak in salted water about 10 minutes until softened, then drain. Peel and cut the ginger root into very thin matchsticks. Mix all the ingredients for the vinegar dressing in a pan and simmer over medium heat a few minutes until the sugar has dissolved. Remove from the heat and let cool.

Place a large sheet of plastic wrap on a cutting board and lay half the fish slices in the center. Spread the ginger shreds and then the cucumber slices evenly on top and sprinkle with the chopped basil leaves. Cover with the remaining fish and wrap with the plastic wrap. Put another board on top and press a few minutes. Unwrap and cut into 2 x 1-inch pieces. Arrange in individual dishes and garnish with lime slices. Serve with small bowls of dressing.

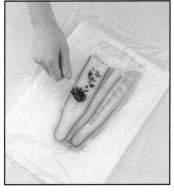

Makes 4 servings.

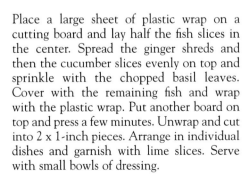

TEMPURA

4 raw jumbo or 8 medium shrimp
12 to 14 oz. whiting fillets
All-purpose flour for coating
4 to 8 fresh shiitake or button mushrooms
8 asparagus tips or okra pods
Vegetable oil for deep-frying
Grated daikon (mooli) and ginger root, to garnish
BATTER:
1 egg yolk, beaten
1 cup ice cold water
1 cup all-purpose flour, sifted
DIPPING SAUCE:
1 cup Dashi, page 12
¼ cup mirin
⅓ cup shoyu

Peel shrimp, retaining tail shell, and devein. Make a few slits along inside curve to prevent curling during cooking. Cut the whiting fillets into pieces about 2 inches long and roll in flour. If the mushrooms are large, cut them in half. Heat the oil for deep-frying to 340F (170C). Meanwhile, prepare the batter: lightly mix the egg yolk with the ice cold water and add the flour at once. Using chopsticks or a fork, very lightly fold in the flour with just 4 or 5 strokes. The batter should be loosely mixed but still very lumpy.

Deep-fry asparagus tips or okra without any batter 2 to 3 minutes, then drain on a wire rack. Dip mushrooms, shrimp (one at a time, holding by tail) and whiting fillets in batter. Deep-fry one at a time in this order 1 to 3 minutes until light golden. Drain them on the rack, then arrange on paper towels on individual plates. Boil the dashi, mirin and shoyu in a pan and pour into small individual bowls. Serve garnished with daikon and ginger.

Makes 4 servings.

FRIED JUMBO SHRIMP

16 raw jumbo shrimp
Salt and sake
2 oz. rice vermicelli
Vegetable oil for deep-frying
All-purpose flour for coating
2 egg whites, lightly beaten
½ cup dried breadcrumbs
Lettuce leaves, to serve
Lemon wedges, to garnish

Peel shrimp, retaining tail shell, and devein.
Make a few slits along inside curve to prevent curling during cooking. Sprinkle with
salt and a little sake and set aside.

Put the vermicelli in a bag and crush into
pieces. Heat oil in a wok or deep-fryer to
about 340F (170C). Holding the tail to
avoid coating the tail shell, dust a shrimp
with flour, coat with egg white and then
with breadcrumbs. Deep-fry 2 to 3 minutes
until golden brown, turning frequently.
Drain on a wire rack. Repeat with another
7 of the shrimp.

Dust the remaining 8 shrimp with flour, coat
with egg white and then dredge in crushed
vermicelli instead of breadcrumbs. Reduce
the oil temperature to 320F (160C) – this
lower temperature helps retain the white-
ness of the vermicelli. Deep-fry the shrimp 2
to 3 minutes, then drain on the wire rack.
Arrange 2 of each type of shrimp on a bed of
lettuce leaves on each of 4 individual plates,
garnish with lemon wedges and serve.

Makes 4 servings.

FRIED FLOUNDER

1 large flounder, filleted
Sake
4 tablespoons cornstarch
Oil for deep-frying
Juice of ½ lemon
1½ tablespoons shoyu
2 tablespoons 'autumn maple leaf' relish', page 28

Cut flounder fillets in half lengthwise and then into 2-inch pieces. Sprinkle with a dash of sake and set aside.

Dredge the flounder pieces in the cornstarch, shaking off any excess. Heat the oil in a wok or a deep-fryer to 320F (160C). Meanwhile, in a small bowl, mix the lemon juice and the shoyu to make a dipping sauce.

Deep-fry the flounder pieces 5 minutes. Increase the heat to raise the temperature of the oil to 340F (170C) and continue frying 2 minutes to make the flounder crispy. Drain on a wire rack. Serve the fried flounder pieces with small individual bowls of the sauce, accompanied by the grated daikon in a small bowl.

Makes 4 servings.

──MACKEREL TATSUTA FRY──

1½ lbs. mackerel, filleted
1 cup cornstarch
Vegetable oil for deep-frying
Lemon wedges, to garnish
MARINADE:
4 tablespoons sake
2 tablespoons shoyu
1-inch piece ginger root, peeled and grated

Remove the large bones from the mackerel fillets. Slice the fillets crosswise into bite-size pieces, inserting the blade diagonally.

In a bowl, combine the ingredients for the marinade. Add mackerel pieces, turning to coat with the marinade, then marinate 30 minutes. Drain and toss the mackerel in the cornstarch to coat thoroughly.

Heat oil in a wok or a deep-fryer to 320F (160C). Slide the mackerel pieces into the hot oil, a few pieces at a time, and fry 2 to 3 minutes until golden brown, turning 2 to 3 times. Remove from the oil and drain on a wire rack. Arrange fried mackerel on each of 4 individual plates, on folded paper towels if desired. Alternatively, heap all the fish in the center of a bamboo basket tray. Garnish with lemon wedges and serve at once.

Makes 4 servings.

—SALMON & NANBAN SAUCE—

1 lb. salmon fillet with skin, scaled
Salt
All-purpose flour for coating
Vegetable oil for deep-frying
3 green onions, shredded, to garnish
NANBAN SAUCE:
4 tablespoons shoyu
3 tablespoons rice vinegar
1½ tablespoons sake
2 teaspoons sugar
4½ tablespoons Dashi, page 12
1 to 2 dried or fresh red chiles, seeded and chopped

Cut the salmon fillet, with skin on, into 12 pieces and sprinkle with a pinch of salt.

Combine all the ingredients for the sauce in a saucepan and bring to a boil. Leave to cool. Pat dry the salmon pieces with paper towels and dredge in flour. Heat oil in a wok or a deep-fryer to 340F (170C). Shake off any excess flour from the salmon pieces and deep-fry 3 to 4 minutes until golden brown. Drain on a wire rack.

Transfer the fried salmon pieces to a large serving plate and spread the shredded green onion on top. Pour sauce over salmon and serve at once.

Makes 4 servings.

SWORDFISH TERIYAKI

2 to 3 swordfish steaks, each weighing about 7 to 9
ounces
6 tablespoons shoyu
2 tablespoons sake
3 tablespoons mirin
4 to 5 fresh mint leaves, chopped
Vegetable oil for frying
Watercress sprigs, to garnish

Slice swordfish steaks in half horizontally to
make a thickness of ½ inch; cut into 2½ x 1½-
inch pieces. In a bowl, mix shoyu, sake, mirin
and mint, then add fish. Mix well and marinate 30 to 40 minutes, turning occasionally.

Heat a frying pan and spread a little oil
evenly over the bottom. Drain the fish
pieces, reserving the marinade and fry a few
pieces at a time over high heat until both
sides become dark brown.

When all the swordfish pieces are cooked
return them to the frying pan. Add marinade, stir to combine and bring to a boil.
Divide mixture between 4 individual plates
or heap it in the center of a serving plate.
Garnish with sprigs of watercress and serve
at once.

Makes 4 servings.

—SALT-SIMMERED SARDINES—

2¼ lbs. sardines, cleaned
Salt
Lemon juice
2-inch piece ginger root, peeled and thinly sliced
2 dried red chiles
⅓ cup sake or white wine
Lime slices, to garnish
LIME SAUCE:
1 lime juice
1 tablespoon shoyu
2 teaspoons mirin

Cut off sardine heads and rinse the bodies under cold running water.

Rinse in salted water (2 quarts water to ½ cup salt). Drain and sprinkle with lemon juice. In a large frying pan or shallow saucepan, spread 2¼ teaspoons salt and half the ginger slices. Lay sardines close together on top. Put the rest of the ginger slices and another 2¼ teaspoons salt on the sardines and add the chiles. Place the pan over medium heat and pour in the sake or wine. When it starts to heat up, add just enough water to cover the sardines. Cut a piece of waxed paper to fit inside the pan and place on sardines.

Remove any residues floating on the surface and when the water is reduced to about one-third, remove the paper. Continue cooking until all the water evaporates (you will hear a sizzling noise) and remove from the heat. Mix all the ingredients for the lime sauce in a small bowl with 1 tablespoon water. Arrange 3-5 sardines on each individual plate, garnish with lime slices and serve with the lime sauce.

Makes 6 to 8 servings.

-CHICKEN WITH WASABI SAUCE-

4 chicken breast fillets, trimmed
1 tablespoon sake
Watercress sprigs and lemon slices, to garnish
WASABI SAUCE:
2 teaspoons wasabi paste or powder
3 tablespoons shoyu
Juice of ½ lemon
1 tablespoon sake or white wine
2 tablespoons chopped fresh chives

Cut each chicken fillet into 2 pieces along its natural line.

Inserting the knife blade diagonally, slice the fillets crosswise into pieces ½-inch thickness. Sprinkle with the sake. To make the wasabi sauce, mix wasabi paste, shoyu, lemon juice, sake or white wine and chopped chives. If using wasabi powder, mix with the same amount of water to make a paste, then mix with sauce ingredients.

Cook the chicken, a few slices at a time, in boiling water 2 minutes (do not overcook), then plunge into ice cold water. Drain the slices and serve on individual plates, garnished with watercress and lemon slices and accompanied by small individual bowls of wasabi sauce.

Makes 4 servings as a starter.

-CHICKEN ROLLED ASPARAGUS-

4 chicken breast fillets
¼ cup sake or white wine
Salt and freshly ground black pepper
12 asparagus tips or 32-40 green beans,
    trimmed
Vegetable oil for frying
1 cup Dashi, page 12, or chicken stock
1 package fresh spinach, trimmed
MUSTARD SAUCE:
2 teaspoons prepared mustard
3 tablespoons shoyu

Cut chicken fillets in half along natural line and slice thickest parts horizontally in half.

By making a few slits on thick parts even out the thickness to make 3 thin flat pieces per chicken breast, about ¼-inch thickness. Sprinkle with a little of the sake and salt and pepper. Parboil the asparagus or green beans in lightly salted water and drain. Place a stalk of asparagus (or 4 to 5 greenbeans) on a chicken piece, roll up and secure with wooden picks. If the asparagus is too long, trim to length of chicken. Repeat with rest of chicken and asparagus or beans. Heat oil in a frying pan and pan-fry chicken rolls until a light golden.

Add rest of sake and the dashi or stock, bring to boil, then simmer 15 minutes. Cook spinach in boiling salted water 1 minute, drain and chop into bite-size lengths. Dissolve mustard with shoyu and add 2 to 3 tablespoons of cooking juices to make a sauce. Cut the chicken rolls into bite-size pieces. Divide the spinach among 4 individual serving plates, heaping it into a nest, pour the sauce over the top, then arrange chicken pieces, cut-side up, on top.

Makes 4 servings.

—CHICKEN & CABBAGE ROLLS—

1 lb. ground chicken
1 tablespoon each miso and shoyu
1 tablespoon sugar
Salt
4 large leaves Savoy cabbage
4 green onions, shredded
Sake
Cooked and shredded carrot, to garnish
MUSTARD SAUCE:
1-2 teaspoons prepared mustard
2 tablespoons shoyu

Mix the minced chicken, miso, shoyu, sugar and a little salt and grind to a smooth paste, using the back of a tablespoon.

Trim the thick part of the central vein on the back of cabbage leaves, then parboil the leaves in lightly salted water. Place one leaf flat on a cutting board, trimmed side up and the bottom of the leaf nearest to you. Spread ¼ of the minced chicken paste evenly over top, leaving about ½-inch margin from the top of the leaf. Arrange ¼ of the green onion shreds crosswise in the center and roll up. Seal the edge with a wooden cocktail pick. Repeat to make 3 more rolls.

Place rolls on a large plate and sprinkle with sake. Place plate in a steamer and steam the rolls over high heat 15 minutes or until chicken meat is well cooked. Drain, remove the cocktail picks and cut each roll diagonally into 4 to 5 pieces. Make a bed of shredded carrot on 4 individual serving plates and arrange the pieces of roll on top. In a cup, mix mustard and shoyu with 2 to 3 tablespoons of cooking juices. Pour sauce over chicken and cabbage and serve at once.

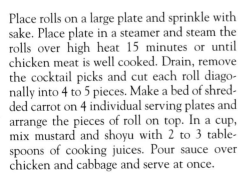

Makes 4 servings as a starter.

—BROILED SKEWERED CHICKEN—

8 chicken thighs, boned
8 green onions, white part only
24 okra, trimmed
Lemon wedges, sansho peppers and chile powder, to
  garnish
SAUCE:
3 tablespoons sake
⅓ cup shoyu
1 tablespoon each mirin and sugar

Cut the chicken thighs into 1-inch square pieces and green onions crosswise into 1-inch lengths. Mix ingredients for the sauce in a saucepan and bring to a boil. Remove from heat and set aside.

If grilling, prepare the grill. Thread 4 pieces of chicken and 3 okra alternately onto an 8-inch bamboo or stainless steel skewer. Repeat with another 7 skewers. Thread another 8 with 4 pieces of chicken and 3 pieces of green onion. Thread any remaining ingredients onto extra skewers. Cook on the grill, keeping the skewer handles well away from the fire and turning them frequently. Brush with the sauce 2 to 3 times during cooking, until the chicken is well cooked and golden brown.

If broiling, preheat broiler. On a well-oiled wire rack, spread chicken pieces well apart and broil until both sides are golden brown. Dip pieces in sauce, put back on rack and broil 30 seconds on each side. Set aside. Lightly broil the green onions and okra without dipping in sauce. Thread 4 chicken pieces alternately with 3 green onions on 8 skewers and with okra on another 8. Serve on a platter, garnished with lemon, sansho peppers and chile powder.

Makes 4-8 servings as a starter.

–CHARBROILED YUAN CHICKEN–

4 whole chicken legs, boned
8 large green onions, white part only
Lime or lemon wedges, to garnish
MARINADE:
⅓ cup sake or white wine
⅓ cup mirin or 1 tablespoon sugar
⅓ cup shoyu
Peel of 1 lemon or lime, in large pieces not chopped
    or shredded

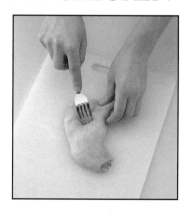

Place the chicken legs on a cutting board
skin side up. Using a fork, pierce the skin in
a few places. Cut the green onions crosswise
into 1½-inch lengths.

In a dish, mix all the marinade ingredients,
add the chicken and green onions and marinate 30 minutes. If grilling, prepare grill.
Thread 3-4 long stainless steel skewers
through each chicken leg parallel with the
skin in a fan shape. Chargrill skin side down,
over high heat 6 to 7 minutes until golden
brown, then turn and cook the other side 3
to 4 minutes. Thread the green onions, 6 to
8 pieces to a skewer, and chargrill. Remove
skewers and serve 1 chicken leg and ¼ of the
green onion on each of 4 individual plates.

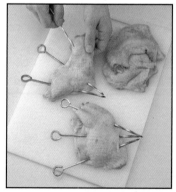

If broiling, preheat broiler. Lay the chicken
legs, unskewered, flat on a wire rack, with
the skin side facing the heat first and broil
about 10 minutes until golden brown. Turn
and broil the other side 5 to 10 minutes until
well cooked. Broil the green onions until
both sides are golden brown. Cut the
chicken legs into bite-size pieces and
arrange the chicken and green onions on 4
individual plates. Serve hot, garnished with
lime or lemon wedges.

Makes 4 servings.

—FRIED FISH-STUFFED CHICKEN—

5-7 oz. cod fillet, skinned
Salt and freshly ground black pepper
4 chicken breast fillets, skinned
All-purpose flour for coating
1 egg, beaten
Dried breadcrumbs
Vegetable oil for deep-frying
Shredded lettuce, to garnish
DIPPING SAUCE:
6 tablespoons mayonnaise
1½ tablespoons shoyu

To make sauce, mix together mayonnaise and shoyu. Set aside. Sprinkle the cod fillet with a pinch of salt and pepper.

Separate one chicken fillet along its natural divide into 2 pieces and cut the larger piece crosswise into 4 pieces and the smaller one into 2 pieces. Slice the 2 thickest pieces horizontally in half to make 8 pieces of even thickness, about ¼ inch. Repeat this with the remaining 3 fillets. Make a deep slit horizontally in the center of each piece to make chicken envelopes and stuff with small pieces of the seasoned cod. The chicken should completely encase the fish.

Dust stuffed chicken with flour, dip into beaten egg, then roll in breadcrumbs and press gently to seal chicken envelope with the breadcrumbs. Heat the oil in a wok or deep-fryer to 340F (170C) and deep-fry the chicken pieces, a few at a time, 5 to 6 minutes until golden brown, turning frequently. Drain on a wire rack or paper towels. Make a bed of shredded lettuce on 4 individual plates. Arrange chicken on top. Serve at once with the sauce.

Makes 4 servings.

—COD ROE-STUFFED CHICKEN—

4 chicken thighs, boned and skinned
5 oz. smoked cod roe
Vegetable oil and butter for frying
Sake or white wine
Parboiled snow peas, to garnish
COD ROE MAYONNAISE:
4 tablespoons mayonnaise
1 tablespoon smoked cod roe, inside only
1 tablespoon prepared mustard

Remove any fat from the chicken thighs and place on a cutting board, skinned side down. Open up the inner side by making several slits lengthwise and even out the thickness.

Cut the cod roe lengthwise into 5 strips and reserve one for making the sauce. Put a strip of cod roe on top of each chicken thigh, placing it lengthwise in the center. Roll in the original thigh shape and seal the end with a wooden pick. Heat a frying pan, add a little vegetable oil and 1 tablespoon butter and fry the stuffed chicken thighs over high heat until both sides are golden brown. Drain on paper towels.

Transfer chicken to a large deep plate, or a shallow dish, and sprinkle generously with sake or white wine. Place the chicken in a steamer and steam 10 to 15 minutes until well cooked. Mix the mayonnaise, remaining cod roe and mustard and place ¼ in the center of each of 4 individual plates. Remove chicken from steamer and drain. Remove picks and place chicken on mayonnaise. Garnish with snow peas and serve.

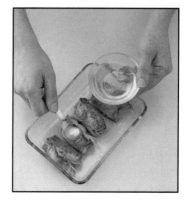

Makes 4 to 6 servings as a starter.

–CHICKEN WITH ONION SAUCE–

8 chicken thighs, boned
Sake, shoyu and sesame oil
1 egg, beaten
9 oz. broccoli, separated into flowerets
Cornstarch for coating
Vegetable oil for deep-frying
Red bell pepper, shredded, to garnish
GREEN ONION SAUCE:
1-2 green onions, finely chopped
2 tablespoons each shoyu and sake or white wine
2 tablespoons mirin or 2 teaspoons sugar
2 teaspoons sesame oil

Cut the chicken, with skin on, into bite-size pieces and put into a large bowl.

Sprinkle generously with sake, shoyu and sesame oil and leave to marinate about 15 minutes. Fold in the beaten egg and leave 15 minutes. Meanwhile, make the green onion sauce by mixing all the ingredients in a bowl. Cook the broccoli in lightly salted boiling water 3 minutes. Drain and keep warm. Roll the chicken pieces in cornstarch and shake off the excess.

Heat vegetable oil in a wok or deep-fryer to 340F (170C) and fry chicken pieces, several at a time, until well cooked and light golden, turning frequently. (Do not add too much chicken at a time – the pan should not be more than two-thirds full at any time.) Drain well on a wire rack or paper towels and arrange in the center of a serving platter along with the broccoli. Pour the sauce over the top, sprinkle with the red bell pepper and serve at once.

Makes 4 servings.

GINGER PORK

1 lb. pork fillets or boneless chops
2-inch piece ginger root, peeled and grated
4 tablespoons shoyu
Boiled rice and lightly cooked snow peas, to garnish

Inserting the blade of a knife diagonally, slice the pork fillets crosswise into very thin rounds. If using chops, discard fat and cut roughly into 2 x 1-inch thin pieces.

Place pork slices on a large plate, spreading as widely apart as possible, and sprinkle all over with the grated ginger, together with its juice, and the shoyu. Marinate 15 minutes.

Heat a frying pan, add 2 to 3 tablespoons vegetable oil and fry the pork slices 2 to 3 minutes on each side until they are well cooked and both sides are golden brown. Arrange the cooked pork slices on a bed of boiled rice, garnish with the snow peas and serve at once.

Makes 4 servings.

FRIED PORK CUTLETS

4 pork loin cutlets or boneless chops
Salt and freshly ground black pepper
All-purpose flour for coating
2 eggs, beaten
Dried breadcrumbs for coating
Vegetable oil for deep-frying
Shredded cabbage and lemon wedges, to garnish
TONKATSU SAUCE:
4 tablespoons tomato ketchup
1 tablespoon shoyu
2 teaspoons Worcestershire sauce
2 teaspoons mustard plus extra for serving

Make a few slits in the cutlet or chop edges to prevent them curling when cooked.

Sprinkle both sides of the pork cutlets with salt and pepper and dredge with flour, shaking off any excess. Dip in the beaten egg, then coat in breadcrumbs. Heat oil in a wok or a deep-fryer to 350F (180C). Gently slide in the pork cutlets, 1 or 2 at a time, and deep-fry 5 to 7 minutes until golden brown, turning once or twice. Drain on paper towels. In between each batch, clean the oil with a mesh ladle. Meanwhile, mix all the ingredients for the sauce in a small serving bowl.

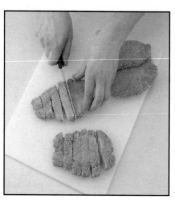

When all the cutlets have been cooked, place them on a cutting board and cut each one crosswise into 1-inch strips. Arrange the cutlets on 4 individual plates and garnish with very finely shredded raw cabbage and lemon wedges. Serve with the sauce and extra mustard, if desired.

Makes 4 servings.

Note: This dish is called Tonkatsu in Japanese.

—PORK WITH CITRUS SHOYU—

1 lb. pork loin or ham
3 green onions, cut in half
2-inch piece ginger root, peeled and cut into 3-4
    pieces
Salt
CITRUS SHOYU:
Juice of ½ lemon
1 tablespoon each lime juice and rice vinegar
2 tablespoons shoyu and ½ tablespoon mirin
2 green onions, finely chopped
1-inch piece ginger root, peeled and finely chopped

In a large pot, put pork, onions, ginger and
and a pinch of salt and cover with water.

Bring to a boil, cover pot and simmer gently
2 hours. Drain the meat, put it in a bowl of
ice cold water and refrigerate until chilled.
Remove the pork from the water, pat dry
and then slice it crosswise against the grain
as thinly as possible. Arrange the slices, fan-
ning them out around the edge of a large
serving platter.

To make the citrus shoyu, mix all the
ingredients together and stir well until the
sugar has dissolved. Transfer it to a serving
bowl or a ramekin and place in the center of
the pork circle. Serve cold.

Makes 4 servings.

—BROILED PORK WITH MISO—

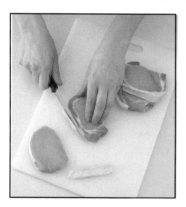

4 pork loin steaks
Lemon wedges, to garnish
MISO SAUCE:
3 tablespoons red miso
3 green onions, finely chopped
2 teaspoons sake
2 teaspoons ginger root juice

Remove any fat from the pork. If the pork is more than ⅔-inch thick, horizontally slice it evenly in half.

Preheat broiler. Heat a well-oiled wire rack under the hot broiler and place the pork steaks on it. Broil the pork 3 to 4 minutes on each side or until both sides are golden brown and well cooked.

In a bowl, make the miso sauce by mixing all the ingredients. Remove the rack from the broiler. Spoon the miso sauce evenly onto the center of the pork steaks and broil farther from the heat 1 minute until the miso sauce is fairly dry. Transfer the steaks to 4 individual plates, garnish with lemon wedges and serve.

Makes 4 servings.

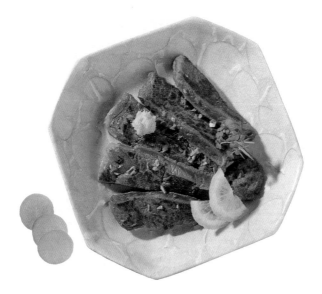

—STEAK WITH GRATED DAIKON—

4 beef fillet or sirloin steaks, about 9 oz. each
Vegetable oil
2 tablespoons butter
Brandy for sprinkling
½ small onion, grated
Shoyu
1 green onion, finely chopped
Cress and lemon slices, to garnish
DAIKON RELISH:
4-inch piece of large daikon, peeled and grated
2 teaspoons wasabi paste

To make relish, lightly squeeze out the water from grated daikon, reserving the water. Put daikon in a bowl and mix in wasabi paste.

With the tip of a blade, cut the edges of the steaks to prevent them from shrinking when cooked. Heat a little oil and ½ tablespoon of butter per steak and fry the steaks, 1 or 2 at a time, to your liking. Sprinkle with a little brandy and flame. When the flames burn out, remove steaks from the pan, cut cross-wise into 2-inch strips and keep warm.

Skim off oil from pan, add grated onion and quickly stir-fry. Pour the reserved water from the grated daikon into the pan and add 2 to 3 tablespoons shoyu. When mixture is warm, put 2 to 3 tablespoons on each of 4 individual plates and place a sliced steak on top. Arrange the daikon relish on the steak and sprinkle with the chopped green onion. Garnish with cress and lemon slices and serve hot.

Makes 4 servings.

—BEEF SALAD WITH EGGPLANT—

1 lb. beef round steak
Salt and freshly ground pepper
1 large eggplant, trimmed
Vegetable oil for deep-frying
5 oz. okra, trimmed
GINGER SHOYU:
2 tablespoons ginger root juice
¼ cup shoyu
3 tablespoons wine vinegar
1 tablespoon sake

Sprinkle the steak with salt and pepper. Cut eggplant into bite-size pieces. Prepare the ginger shoyu by mixing all the ingredients together, then set aside.

Heat vegetable oil in a wok or a deep-fryer to about 340F (170C) and quickly deep-fry eggplant pieces and whole okra about 1 minute. Drain on paper towels.

Heat a frying pan and add a little vegetable oil. Add steak and fry on high heat until both sides are golden brown and cooked to your liking. Turn out on to a slightly damp cutting board, leave to cool and cut in half lengthwise and then crosswise into ¼-inch-thick slices. Put the steak, eggplant and okra in a large serving bowl, pour over the ginger shoyu and toss well. Serve warm or chilled.

Makes 4 to 6 servings.

BEEF TERIYAKI

5-7 oz. asparagus tips
Salt
½ cup Dashi, page 12
4 tablespoons shoyu
4 beef sirloin or round steaks, about 9 oz. each
Vegetable oil
4 tablespoons sake or white wine
3 tablespoons mirin or 1 tablespoon sugar
Mustard, to serve

Boil asparagus tips in lightly salted water 3 minutes, drain, cool under cold running water and pat dry. In a bowl, mix the dashi and 2 tablespoons of the shoyu, pour it over asparagus and leave to marinate.

Lightly salt the steaks and fry in a little oil over high heat, covered, 3 minutes on one side. Turn over and while second side is frying sprinkle the meat with 1 tablespoon sake or white wine per steak. Cover the pan and fry 2 to 3 minutes. Remove the steaks to a plate.

Add the remaining shoyu and the mirin or sugar to the pan and mix with the meat cooking juices. Return the steaks to the pan and coat them on both sides with the teriyaki sauce. Turn out on to a cutting board and cut the steaks crosswise into ⅔-inch slices. Arrange the steaks on individual plates and spoon over some teriyaki sauce. Garnish with the asparagus tips and serve with mustard.

Makes 4 servings.

BEEF TATAKI

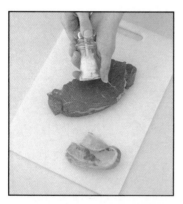

1 lb. lean beef sirloin steak
Salt and vegetable oil for brushing
2 green onions, finely chopped
1-inch piece ginger root, peeled and grated
1 tablespoon wasabi paste
½ cucumber
Lime slices and watercress, to garnish
DAIKON DIP:
3-inch daikon (mooli), peeled and grated
3 tablespoons shoyu
Juice of ½ lime

Preheat broiler. Trim fat from meat, sprinkle with a pinch of salt and brush with oil.

Quickly brown meat under a hot broiler 2 to 3 minutes on each side. Remove from the heat and immediately plunge into ice cold water to stop further cooking. Traditionally the meat should be golden brown outside but rare inside. Drain, pat dry and set aside while preparing the daikon dip. Mix the grated daikon, shoyu and lime juice in a serving bowl. Arrange the chopped green onions, grated ginger and wasabi in separate heaps on a small plate. Cut the cucumber in half lengthwise, then slice crosswise into paper- thin half-moons.

Slice the meat very thinly across the grain. Arange each piece folded on a half-moon slice of cucumber, slightly overlapping in a circle on a large serving platter. Garnish with lime slices and watercress. Serve with the bowl of daikon dip, accompanied by the plate of condiments. Each diner has a small plate for mixing individual dip sauces.

Makes 4 to 6 servings.

Note: Serve this dish with grated chile-daikon mixture, see page 28, if liked.

—SIMMERED BEEF & POTATOES—

10-oz. piece lean beef
5 medium potatoes, peeled
2 onions
2 tablespoons vegetable oil
5 tablespoons sugar
6 tablespoons shoyu
Dashi, page 12, or water
Parboiled snow peas, to garnish

Put the beef in the freezer about 1 hour to partially freeze, then slice very thinly across the grain into bite-size pieces.

Quarter each potato and boil until tender but still slightly hard in the center. Drain and set aside. Cut the onions into thin half-moon slices. In a frying pan or a shallow saucepan, heat a little vegetable oil and stir-fry the beef slices over medium heat. When the beef begins to change color, add the potatoes and continue to stir. Add the sugar and shoyu to the pan and lightly stir in. Pour in enough dashi or water to just cover the ingredients and bring to a boil. Skim the surface and reduce the heat.

Place a small wooden lid or a plate touching the ingredients inside the pan and simmer over medium heat 10 minutes. Add the onion slices and continue to cook until all ingredients are tender and have absorbed the flavor. Serve in small individual bowls garnished with snow peas.

Makes 4 servings.

MIXED HOT POT

10 oz. beef sirloin or 2 chicken breast fillets,
  skinned
1 squid, cleaned (optional)
4-8 scallops or raw jumbo shrimp, peeled
4-8 fresh shiitake or button mushrooms, stalks
  removed
1 red or green bell pepper, seeded
9 oz. bean sprouts, trimmed
1 lemon, cut into wedges
2-3 green onions, finely chopped
Vegetable oil for frying
DIPPING SAUCE:
6-inch daikon (mooli), peeled
1 fresh or dried chile
Shoyu

Prepare wafer-thin beef slices following the
method used for Sukiyaki, opposite. Skin
the squid by holding the 2 flaps together and
peeling down; cut in half lengthwise. Put
squid fillets on a cutting board skinned-side
up and make fine cross cuts on them with a
sharp knife. Cut fillets and flaps into 1-inch
square pieces. Separate the tentacles, if
large. Arrange meat and seafood on separate
platters. If the mushrooms are large, cut
them in half. Slice the bell pepper into thin
strips. Arrange all vegetables on a platter.

Make grated chile-daikon mixture following
the method on page 28, or, grate the daikon,
finely chop the fresh chile and simply mix
together. Arrange daikon mixture , lemon
wedges and the green onion in a serving
bowl or on small plate. Place a hotplate
in the center of the dining table set with small
individual bowls. Serve the meat, fish and
vegetable   platters   and   condiments:
diners mix their own sauce, adding shoyu to
taste, and fry their portion for themselves.

Makes 4 to 6 servings.

—SUKIYAKI (PAN-COOKED BEEF)—

1 lb. sirloin or topside of beef
2 leeks, white part only
8 fresh or dried shiitake or button mushrooms,
   stalks removed if fresh
Sugar
9 oz. (1 cake) tofu
4 oz. watercress, trimmed
2-inch square of beef fat
⅓ cup sake or white wine
¼ cup shoyu

Trim off any fat from the beef and cut the beef into 3 x 1½-inch flat pieces (any length).

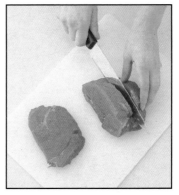

Place in separate freezer bags and freeze 1 to 2 hours. Take out of freezer and leave until half-thawed. Cut the beef into wafer-thin slices and arrange in a circular fan on a large platter. Slice the leeks diagonally. If the shiitake mushrooms are large, cut in half. If using dried shiitake, soak in warm water with a pinch of sugar 45 minutes, then remove stems. Cut the tofu into 16 cubes. Arrange all the vegetables and tofu on a large platter.

Place a cast-iron skillet on a portable gas ring or electric hotplate on the table together with the platters of raw ingredients, cups of water, the shoyu and sake and a sugar bowl. Melt the beef fat in the pan and move around to oil the entire bottom. Cook a few slices of beef first, then add some of the other ingredients and sprinkle with about 2 tablespoons sugar. Pour in the sake and shoyu, and add water to taste. Diners serve themselves into individual small bowls.

Makes 4 servings.

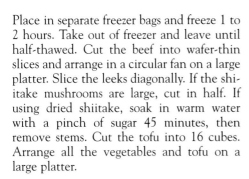

–SHABUSHABU (BEEF HOT POT)–

1 lb. beef sirloin
2 leeks, white part only
8 fresh or dried shiitake or 12 button mushrooms,
  stalks removed
9 oz. (1 cake) firm tofu
4-6 Chinese cabbage (hakusai) leaves
1 package fresh spinach, trimmed
4-inch piece dried konbu (kelp)
10 oz. udon noodles, cooked (optional)
Finely chopped green onion, to garnish
CITRUS DIP:
½ daikon (mooli), peeled
1 dried or fresh red chile
2 green onions, finely chopped
Juice of ½ lemon and ½ lime
½ cup shoyu

SESAME DIP:
4 tablespoons sesame paste or smooth peanut butter
½ cup Dashi, page 12
3 tablespoons shoyu
1 tablespoons mirin or sweet sherry
1 tablespoon sugar
2 tablespoons sake or white wine
2 teaspoons chile oil or chile powder (optional)

Trim off any fat from the beef and cut into 3
x 1½-inch flat pieces (any length). Place in
separate freezer bags and freeze 1 to 2 hours.

Remove from the freezer and leave until half
thawed, then cut the beef into wafer-thin
slices and arrange in a circular fan on a large
platter. Slice leeks diagonally. If the shiitake
mushrooms are large cut in half. If using
dried shiitake, soak in warm water with a
pinch of sugar 45 minutes, then remove
stems before use. Cut the tofu into 16 cubes.
Cut the Chinese cabbage leaves and spinach
into bite-size pieces. Arrange the vegetables
and tofu on a large platter.

To prepare the citrus dip, first make grated chile-daikon mixture, following the method on page 28. Or, grate the daikon very finely and chop the fresh red chile, then mix together. Put daikon mixture, chopped green onions, lemon and lime juices and the shoyu in separate small bowls. To make the sesame dip, mix all the ingredients together and stir until the sesame paste (or peanut butter) is of a smooth runny consistency. Divide among 4 to 6 individual dipping bowls.

Put the konbu in a large pot (ideally a clay pot, an enameled cast-iron pot or a copper-based Mongolian hotpot) and fill two-thirds full with water. Bring to a boil and remove the konbu. Put in some of the leek, Chinese cabbage, shiitake mushrooms, spinach and tofu and when it begins to come back to boil, transfer the pot to a portable gas ring or electric hotplate on the dining table. Diners make their own citrus dip in individual dipping bowls by mixing 1 to 2 teaspoons each of each ingredient with some shoyu.

Diners serve themselves by cooking the meat in the pot, adding more vegetables, and eating them dipped in either of the sauces. When ingredients are finished, skim and season the soup with shoyu and a little salt and sugar. If using noodles, warm them in the soup, seasoned with a little shoyu to taste, so that diners can end the meal with plain noodles garnished with chopped green onion.

Makes 4 to 6 servings.

——TOFU & FISH HOT POT——

1 lb. 2oz. (2 cakes) tofu
9 oz. white fish steak or fillets, such as cod
4 Chinese cabbage (hakusai) leaves
2 oz. cilantro leaves and/or 7 oz. spinach, trimmed
2-3 green onions, finely chopped
SOUP:
6-inch piece dried konbu (kelp) (optional)
2½ cups Dashi, page 12
3 tablespoons shoyu
½ tablespoon sugar

Cut the tofu into bite-size cubes and the fish steaks or fillets into chunks with the bone and skin still on.

Cut the Chinese cabbage in half lengthwise and then crosswise into 1-inch long pieces. Chop the cilantro leaves and/or spinach roughly into 2-inch lengths.

To make the soup, put the konbu in a pot (ideally a clay pot or enameled pot) and add the dashi, shoyu and sugar. bring to a boil and then add some of each of the prepared ingredients. When it begins to boil again, transfer pot to a portable gas ring or electric hotplate on the dining table. Diners then serve themselves to some soup and ingredients in individual bowls, sprinkled with chopped green onions.

Makes 4 servings.

ISHIKARI HOT POT

4 salmon steaks with skin , scaled
1 onion
2 potatoes and 1 or 2 carrots
4-8 fresh shiitake or button mushrooms
2 oz. cilantro leaves or watercress
9 oz. (1 cake) firm tofu
10 oz. (1 cake) konnyaku (optional)
2 tablespoons butter
4-inch piece dried konbu (kelp) (optional)
3-5 tablespoons miso
2 green onions, finely chopped

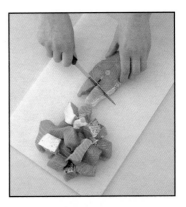

Leaving the skin on, cut the salmon steaks into chunky pieces. Cut onion in half and slice into ¼-inch-thick half-moons.

Slice potatoes and carrots into ½-inch-thick rounds (if large, cut into half-moons) and parboil separately. Drain and set aside. Slice the shiitake mushrooms diagonally into 4 slices. Chop cilantro leaves or watercress into 2½ -inch lengths. Cut the tofu and konnyaku, if using, in half lengthwise, then cut the tofu into ½-inch squares and the konnyaku into ¼-inch slices. Melt butter in a large cast-iron pot and stir-fry onion slices 1 to 2 minutes. Add konbu and enough water to half fill pot.

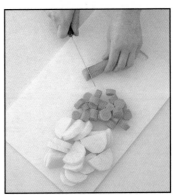

Bring to a boil over medium heat, discard konbu and lower heat. Dissolve the miso in a bowl with some of soup, then stir back into pan. Add potatoes, carrots, salmon, mushrooms and konnyaku, then cover and cook over low heat 5 minutes. Add cilantro or watercress and tofu; simmer 3 to 4 minutes. Serve sprinkled with chopped green onions.

Makes 4 to 6 servings.

Note: Ishikari is a river on the northern island of Japan which is famous for salmon.

—SUMO WRESTLERS' HOT POT—

3¼-3½ lb. whole chicken
4-inch piece dried konbu (kelp) (optional)
9-10 oz. whole fish, such as trout
6 Chinese cabbage (hakusai) leaves
2 carrots
12-18 raw jumbo shrimp, peeled
12-18 shiitake or button mushrooms, stems
   removed
9 oz. broccoli, separated into flowerets
12 mochi rice cakes (optional)
CITRUS DIP:
½ daikon (mooli), peeled
2 dried or fresh red chiles
2 green onions, finely chopped
Juice of 1 lemon and ½ lime
6 tablespoons shoyu

Cut the chicken, including skin and bones, into 1½-2-inch square pieces and wash in boiling water. Drain and put in a large pot. Add the konbu, if using, and half fill the pot with water. bring to a boil over high heat, remove the konbu and simmer the chicken 30 minutes, occasionally skimming off any scum from the surface of the liquid. Meanwhile, scale the fish and cut roughly into 2-inch long chunky pieces. Cut the Chinese cabbage into bite-size pieces and the carrots into thin rounds. Arrange all the ingredients on a platter.

To prepare citrus dip, make grated chile-daikon mixture, following the method on page 28, and put in a serving bowl with the chopped green onions. In a cup, mix the lemon and lime juices and shoyu. Transfer the chicken hot-pot to a portable gas ring or electric hotplate on the dining table set with individual dipping bowls and the citrus dip ingredients. Diners make their own dip and serve themselves.

Makes 6 to 8 servings.

─ODEN─

10 oz. (1 cake) konnyaku
½ daikon (mooli), peeled
1-2 turnips
2-3 potatoes
12 fish balls or cakes
4 eggs, hard-cooked and shelled
Mustard for serving
SOUP:
2½ cups chicken stock
2½ cups Dashi, page 12
½ cup shoyu
½ cup mirin or sake and 2 tablespoons sugar
1 teaspoon salt

Cut konnyaku cake in half, then diagonally quarter each half to make 8 triangles. Cut daikon and turnips in half lengthwise, then into 1-inch-thick half-moon slices. Cook chicken and turnips in boiling water until tender and drain. Cut potatoes in half, or quarter them if large, and parboil. To make soup, in a large earthenware pot or a flame-proof casserole dish, heat the chicken stock and dashi over low heat, then add shoyu and mirin or sake and salt.

Add konnyaku triangles, vegetables, fish balls and eggs and simmer, uncovered, 1 hour. Bring the cooking pot to the dining table for diners to help themselves. Serve with mustard.

Makes 4 servings.

Note: There are many types of ready-to-cook oden ingredients, such as fish balls and cakes, in packages at Japanese supermarkets.

RICE BALLS

2 cups short-grain rice
Salt
5½ oz. salmon steak
2 oz. smoked cod roe, skinned
2 teaspoons sake
Red chile powder (optional)
2 tablespoons black or white sesame seeds
1-2 sheets of nori (wafer-thin dried seaweed),
    optional
Chinese Cabbage & Chiles, page 32, to garnish

Boil rice following the method on page 17. Heavily salt the salmon and leave 30 minutes. Preheat broiler.

Wipe off the salt from the salmon with paper towels and broil salmon under high heat until both sides are lightly burned. Remove the skin and break flesh into rough flakes. Put cod roe in a small bowl, sprinkle with the sake and make into a paste. Add a pinch of chile powder, if desired. Toss sesame seeds in a small saucepan over high heat until fragrant. Place a sheet of nori over low heat and swiftly turn over a few times to bring out the flavor. Using kitchen scissors, cut it into 8 pieces. Repeat if using a second sheet.

Put 2 tablespoons rice into each of 4 wet teacups. Make a hole in center of each, put 1 teaspoonful salmon into each one and press to cover with rice. Wet hands and rub with salt. Turn out rice onto your hand and squeeze, shaping it into a round. Sprinkle with sesame seeds and partly wrap with nori. Make 4 more with cod roe inside but with no sesame seeds. Mix remaining rice and ingredients to make 4 or 5 rice balls. Garnish with cabbage and serve.

Makes about 12.

CHESTNUT RICE

2 cups short-grain rice
1½ teaspoons salt
2 tablespoons sake
5 oz. fresh chestnuts, shelled and peeled or 9 oz.
   cooked peeled chestnuts
Lightly toasted black sesame seeds, to garnish

Put the rice in a deep enameled cast-iron pot and wash well, changing the water several times until the water becomes clear. Leave to soak in just enough water to cover the rice 1 hour. If using fresh chestnuts, cut them in half and gently rinse in cold water. Drain and place on top of rice.

In a measuring cup, dissolve salt with 1 cup water and add to pan. Add extra water, if necessary, to make water level 1 inch above the rice and chestnuts. Pour in the sake, cover and cook over high heat 8 to 10 minutes until mixture begins to sizzle. Reduce heat and simmer 10 minutes until water is absorbed. Let stand, covered, 10 to 15 minutes, then gently mix chestnuts into rice. Serve in rice bowls sprinkled with sesame seeds.

If using cooked chestnuts, cut large ones in half. In a measuring cup, dissolve salt with 1 cup water and add to rice. Add extra water, if necessary, to make the level ⅔ inch above rice. Pour in the sake, cover and cook over high heat 7 to 8 minutes until mixture sizzles. Reduce heat, add chestnuts and simmer, covered, 10 minutes until water is absorbed. Let stand, still covered, 10 to 15 minutes. Gently mix the chestnuts into rice and serve as above.

Makes 4 to 6 servings.

—BABY CLAM RICE—

3 cups short-grain rice
2 tablespoons sake or white wine
2 tablespoons shoyu
1 teaspoon sugar
1 (9-oz.) can baby clams, drained
⅔ teaspoon salt
2 green onions, finely shredded

Put the rice in a deep enameled cast-iron pot and wash well, changing the water several times until the water becomes clear. Leave to soak in just enough water to cover the rice 1 hour.

Meanwhile, in a saucepan, mix sake, shoyu and sugar over high heat and quickly toss in the clams. Skim surface and remove from heat. Pour juice from pan into a measuring cup and keep the clams warm in the pan.

Drain rice. Add enough water to cup to make pan juices up to 1 cup and dissolve the salt in it. Pour mixture over the rice, cover and place on high heat. Bring to boil and cook 7 to 8 minutes until it sizzles, then reduce heat and simmer 10 minutes. Place clams and green onions on top. Cover and cook over high heat 2 seconds. Remove from heat and let stand 10 to 15 minutes. Gently mix clams and green onions into the rice. Serve in rice bowls.

Makes 4 to 6 servings.

TEMPURA RICE BOWL

3 cups short-grain rice
12 raw jumbo shrimp
12 okra, trimmed
1 egg
1 cup all-purpose flour
Vegetable oil for deep-frying
SAUCE:
2 tablespoons sugar
3 tablespoons shoyu
½ cup Dashi, page 12

Boil rice following method on page 17 and keep warm. Peel shrimp, retaining tail shell, and devein. Make a slit along inner curve to prevent curling during cooking.

To make sauce, dissolve sugar with the dashi and shoyu in a saucepan over medium heat and set aside. Beat egg in a measuring cup and add enough water to make up to 1 cup. Add the flour to the cup and gently fold in a few times: do not stir as the batter should be lumpy. Heat oil in a wok or deep-fryer to 340F (170C). Plunge the shrimp and okra, one or two at a time, into the batter and deep-fry until light golden. Drain on paper towels.

Divide the rice among 4 large individual bowls. Pour about 1 tablespoon of the sauce over each portion. Arrange 3 shrimp and 3 okra on top of each portion of rice and pour the remaining sauce over the top. Serve hot.

Makes 4 servings.

Note: Cold left-over tempura, see page 46, can be used for this dish. Gently reheat the tempura in the sauce before placing it on top of boiled rice.

—CHICKEN & EGG RICE BOWL—

3 cups short-grain rice
2 chicken breast fillets
Vegetable oil for frying
2 onions, halved and sliced
4 eggs
Cress, to garnish
COOKING SAUCE:
Salt and 1 cup Dashi, page 12
1 tablespoon sake or white wine
2 tablespoons each shoyu and sugar

Boil the rice following method on page 17 and keep warm. Cut chicken fillets in half along natural dividing line and thinly slice crosswise, inserting knife blade diagonally.

In a saucepan, heat all the sauce ingredients over medium heat until sugar has dissolved. Remove from the heat and set aside. Place a small frying pan over high heat and spread a little oil over the bottom, then fry ¼ of the chicken slices about 2 minutes or until both sides are a light golden brown. Add ¼ of the onion slices and stir-fry 1 minute.

Pour ¼ of the cooking sauce into the pan and when hot, beat an egg and pour over it. Cover and cook until egg hardens. Divide boiled rice among 4 large individual bowls. With a spatula, turn out chicken and egg mixture over bowl of boiled rice and top with some sauce. Repeat this 3 more times to make 4 individual chicken and egg rice bowls. Serve hot, garnished with cress.

Makes 4 servings.